James Madison 1758-1836 Is he a hypocrite or not? By Dove Night M.A.

Montpelier, his estate

Table of contents

A.James Madison , Father of theConstitution

James Madison was pivotal to the passage of the United States Constitution. He reported by observers to have spoken hundreds of times there, and his contemporaries there rated him highly. He written several notes at the Constitutional convention which became the official record for the 1787 convention. He helped gotten the newly formed constitution enacted with the 13 states by offering and giving wise statements by stating that “ men are not angels”, and that the constitution is best because it can help prevent tyranny and prevent the formation of a monarchy. He worked with the north and the south on working on the formation of this legal document, which was enacted due to the disorganization and lack of cohesive government with the articles of confederation. He is now known as the

"Father of the United States Constitution"

James Madison

B. James Madison, the 4th president

James Madison had an excellent record and portfolio for public service. He was a United states representative. He was a statesman, He also was a secretary of state.

His tenure as the fourth president of the United states was an interesting one. He will always be known for the “war of 1812 “when his foreign policy relationship with Britain deteriorated due to the lack of cooperation between he two countries over the theft and sabotage of American ships in the Atlantic Ocean. This involved the British sabotaging ships by attacking them and taking the navy soldiers in their custody. The breakdown of the relations continued until Madison and the United states government wanted to go to war with Britain. When the war happened, The British invaded American, tore through towns and destroy Washington D.C., including the US capitol and the white house. The government and many occupants within the city y had to be evacuated. Dolly Madison, who was the white house, before the British invaded it, had left with the famous Gilbert Stuart portrait of George Washington in 1814. Outside of this, James Madison’s administration saw the decline of the federalist party, and it also had an Indian policy which showed Madison paternalistic views toward Indians (or racist views, perhaps due to the times back in the early 19th century. Madison saw the expiration of the Bank services and after the war of 1812, and the peace between Britain. Madison was reelected to a second term.

C. James Madison as a slaveowner

James Madison was born on a rich Virginia plantation in which he inherited hundreds of slaves from his father. Montpelier, which located near Orange county Virginia and not far from Monticello, was a plantation where slaves worked on and they grew tobacco, corn and other crops. James Madison view slavery as a necessary form of life for his plantation economy yet he felt that the practice was not ethical. James Madison views on slavery philosophical versus his views on slavery economical was hypocritical but he was a man of his times. His involvement with the 3/5 clause that was enacted in the United states constitution showed his conflicting hypocrisy with the slavery issue. Madison, along with Jefferson ,Washington and other founding fathers in the southern United states were not essentially consistent with their view points on slavery, Madison supported promote policies that ended the practice but he continued owning slaves in which he enjoyed the riches that come from it , at the expense of slaves.

Montpelier, the estate of James Madison where he owned slaves

We the People

Article 1

D. Is James Madison a hypocrite

James Madison was a very gifted man, who help transformed a nation whose economical stance was owned and supported by England into a new independent country with a belief and strength to stand on its own. His service in government and his participation in the United states Constitution will always be part of American culture, history and ideas. His ownership of slaves and the conflicting viewpoints on it will unfortunately be a part of America's history and folklore permanently. We can see the hypocrisy in his ideas about freedom, racism which has and will always tarnish him, but his life in politics and government will always be remembered as well. In other words, like the other founding fathers, or at least most of them. James Madison was a man of his times, hypocrite in one way, and brilliant in another.

www.ingramcontent.com/pod-product-compliance
Ingram Content Group UK Ltd.
Pitfield, Milton Keynes, MK11 3LW, UK
UKHW041901190726
13854UKWH00003B/1018

9 780359 002634